If You Want Thunder

If You Want Thunder

Ruth Valentine

Smokestack Books
1 Lake Terrace, Grewelthorpe,
Ripon HG4 3BU
e-mail: info@smokestack-books.co.uk
www.smokestack-books.co.uk

Poems copyright
Ruth Valentine, 2021
all rights reserved.

ISBN 9781838198848

Smokestack Books
is represented by
Inpress Ltd

*for Tzeggai,
regardless*

Contents

Past   9

I Sea-Fret
   Jettisoned   13
   Journey's End   14
   Lamentations   15
   Sound Barrier   16
   Spite   17
   Endangered   18
   What It's About   19

II
   Like Tolstoy   23
   Purple   25
   Cobalt Variations   27
   Alabaster   33
   Smoke   34
   Afterwards   36
   The Calabash   38
   Transhumance   39
   On the Esplanade   40
   The Inshore Waters   41

III
   Commander in Chief   47
   What I Am Saying   48
   During the Bombing of Aleppo   49
   The Martyrs of the Iran–Iraq War   50
   Hostile Environment   51
   Dawn Chorus   52
   A Temporary Cease-Fire Has Been Negotiated 53
   The River at Tottenham Hale, Below Ferry Lane 54
   Today, Tomorrow   56

IV

A Grenfell Alphabet — 61

V Lethe

Not Like This — 73
Before We Knew — 74
Prometheus — 75
Bees — 76
Redevelopment — 77
Pigeon Post — 78
Ghost Station — 80
Intertidal — 82

VI

Tidal — 85
Moorings — 86
If You Want Thunder — 87
Self-Portrait with Skull — 88
Grünewald — 89
One Day the Poets Will Return to Earth — 91
For Eavan Boland — 92
The Painted Sky — 93
The Aralqum Desert — 94
Sonnet Written with a Pink Pen — 97
The Boatman — 98

Notes — 99
Acknowledgments — 101

Past

Walk from the gatehouse – grey stone, Gothic windows,
a rusting padlock – between cypresses
to darkness. Goodbye, strangers' kindnesses,
the offerings of streetlamps. Past the willow,
at night a drift of harp-strings, past the graves
of those who gave up sooner, those who tried
and never made it, those who did, and died
leaving no chronicle. An angel waves
a despairing hand at mud. You mustn't ponder
lead coffins, plague-pits, skeletons. Your task
is *keep on walking.* As the silence grows,
your mind renounces thought. Your body knows
it may not manage all your mind will ask,
and that could be your catastrophe, your wonder.

I
Sea-Fret

Jettisoned

on the passage between the islands the boat was clutched
in the hands of drowned farmers, who pulled it down
into the wave's ploughed furrows, bellowing
my carrots fresh from the earth? where are my oxen?

in the hands of drowned merchants with topaz rings,
fingers of fishermen clawing through the traps
of their lobster-pots

                                      the wild boat shook them off
and headed out to the plain of cormorants
folding themselves like paper, plunging down
to the wrecks and the jetsam, all the jettisoned,

whoever steps awkwardly away from land,
unborn children venturing on an ocean
though grandmothers weep and the soldiers shrug and yawn

Journey's End

Don't think the sea objects to your arrival.
You have as little
say as the scrap of paper someone folds
into a fishing-boat
                places
                        on the water's edge to lurch
                      out past the harbour wall
    until the waves
assume it's another seabird
bend it under.

                *

The sea is a pagan goddess, always hungry.
She tosses you hand to hand like a bruised apple.
    You can write
odes to her fine white horses, you can plead
lost childhood, lost child, lost memory:
    she is not
a court of appeal. You can walk
the shingle barefoot: she won't give absolution.

                *

Truth is, you envy the tide the way it breaks
over sea-walls and sea-defences, concrete blocks
spoiled into the beach.
Sometimes it leaves a mine
at low tide, unexploded, a reminder.
Sometimes it leaves a body, blanched and bloated.

                *

This is your deep ambition, to be found
at dawn at the winter solstice, on the sand,
sightless soundless innocent among
tangles of fishing-line, broken lobster-pots,
sea-lettuce, indigo razor-shells, shards of plastic.

Lamentations

a thin drizzle or sea-fret   absent-minded
something chugging   throbbing   a pile-driver
building a platform of yellow gorse   a thrum

out there the sea's membrane like cooling milk
lift it off with a tablespoon   peer in

*

there was a man crossing between the cliffs
the west wind grabbed him by the coat pockets
and swung him down
now he's come back to tell
encounters in the cave of lamentations

but his jaw has fallen off to become a rock
and catch at the painted keels of lobster-boats
haul them into his inlet make them welcome

Sound Barrier

someone pray to the god who never answers
who never exists   or only in jagged moments
when the sun covers the sea in silver-leaf
and the Icarus wind falls into the water

to become low tide   someone
intone a prayer   for what   a stick of light
prodding down through the sea-fret   a voice a voice

in the walled garden
a cowslip   it's December   fainting flowers

shall we make it an omen
a guarantee of fortune   a recollection

beechwoods in spring   an invisible plane
above the leaf-light   cuts through a barrier
the sound floating to earth like cluster-bombs

Spite

the sea beats at the rock-door with thin white hands
shouting why did you disown me   take me back

the cave   too old to answer   blocks its ears
with mine-spoil bird-shit   no-one can bear to hear

the sea shrieking revenge   overturning ferries
snatching a child off a cliff and twirling him

in swaddling-clothes of spindrift   holding him
tight like a mascot   flinging him into pieces

flint-axes   silver
coins   the face scoured off into history

until even the tide begins to tire
its voice grown hoarse   its memory uncertain

Endangered

words have been trodden in with the sheep-droppings
tangled in gorse protected from wrens by thorns

blown off the land-bridge into the silver mines
swept out to sea dived for by cormorants

loaded on tractors carried onto the ferry
and never returned stolen by sightseers

swapped on the sand by greedy schoolchildren
skimped on the airwaves mocked on the internet

ignored in their stone cottage till the stars
peered between roof-tiles saw there was no-one there

What It's About

A downhill path, muddy, with leaves sodden,
patches of moss, gorse thorns. A clack like linen:
pheasant powering away.
You've never been here.

Rage of the sea searching among its rocks
and never finding its child. The sea-engraving
cross-hatched, shaded. Wind etching its thoughts
on the steel plate of the water. You can keep
the print forever.
Then the haar floats in.

*

Like leaning over a well.
Like standing out in the cold until the stars
and then never enough of them. Like seeing

steps cut into the rockface leading down
to a crescent beach   the first barraged in gorse
the last metres above the sand. Like watching

the Russian pianist dead thirty years
touching the next turn in the fugue and smiling.
Like following the silk cord of a poem

deeper and tighter into the labyrinth
where something paces and groans   until you reach
a granite wall, the end of the cord, fraying.

II

Like Tolstoy

Not in hospital; nobody wants that.
Nor the pale-blue rooms and communal eating-spaces
of the hospice, however kindly. Not alone
on an industrial estate in Switzerland,
being filmed stating *Yes I understand
if I drink this liquid...* Not even in bed at home
surrounded by sobbing family, Victorian
fantasy of reunion and forgiveness.
Since it's going to happen and won't be dignified,
you could do a lot worse than a railway station
waiting-room. Say Barnham, where after class
with the boys from the boys' school we dawdled for the connection:
coal fire, view of the station pub, a playground,
mourners hurrying up from the underpass.

*

I've certainly known some beautiful railway stations.
St Pancras before it became a shopping-mall
and they hid the trains: wood-panelled ticket office,
six empty tracks leading the mind north
past the gasometers to an improbable
state of grace; or Milan with its Day Hotel
where you could have a change of clothes, a shower,
then off to meet Leonardo, your Last Supper.
But the number one station for dying in
must be Ljubljana: the driving snow, the boys
off to art college in Venice, the gun-metal
socialist-realist trains, their sides announcing
the life beyond: Budapest, Bucharest,
Prague, Skopje, Thessaloníki, Athens.

*

You're not taking this seriously. It's not about
childhood or tourism or the early years
of your marriage. You are deciding where to die,
assuming you have a choice and aren't knocked down
by a single-decker bus at Turnpike Lane,
or a heart attack in the Parkways ladies' toilets.
It's losing control of your body, shamefully,
and your mind, which will stop writing poetry forever.
So what you need is less the architecture
(though a final view of a vaulted wrought-iron roof
would do for transcendence) than the sound of trains
leaving for cities you can dream about
in your last minutes, and busy humanity
with its suitcases and phones, its sudden weeping.

Purple

In the echo under the railway-bridge, it's sometimes
hard to tell the wail of the mouth-organ,
a busker standing in shadow, from the brakes,
impatient lorry returning to Rotterdam
empty, the driver hungry. In the cleaner's
a man remembers a woman's suit, along
rails of clinging polythene: *This colour.*

– *A trouser suit or a skirt suit?* It's the lines
carved on his face don't let him understand,
the dark under his eyes. *A suit.*
I've got to take it to the undertaker,
I'm sending the body home.
– *Give me two days,* says Ranjit, but the man

has run out of days to give. If he had days
he'd take them with the suitcase and radio
and give them back to his wife. Two April days,
not enough, but she could have looked out of the window
down on the traffic, the people; there might have been
a few hours' sunshine, sky almost the blue
of the sky back home. *You got nobody to help you?*
he asks, and Ranjit tells him that's the trouble,
maybe this afternoon, if he comes back
at three; it means hunting through the basement,

no date, no receipt. Ranjit's a good man,
his parents have retired, he opens early,
sees to the cleaning, takes in shoe-repairs
for the brothers who had the shop next door, where now
McDonalds draws in men from the fire-engines.
Ranjit tells me, *She died two weeks ago.*
He's been right there, upstairs, and now he wants
a suit she brought in last autumn, all the while
unfolding my kimono, holding it up –
he's tall – above the counter, so I wonder,

the woman who died, sitting
in her room over McDonalds, if she'd have liked
a purple kimono, if she might have felt
better wrapping the silk against the soft
skin of her breasts, if anything could have saved her.

Cobalt Variations

reclusive   not tracked down
in mountains chalkdowns streams

too barbarous
to breathe our air   hidden

among nickel and copper
the malleable the brazen

indifferent god
arriving in the hold of a meteorite

not at the time we pray
at the time we are hollowed

In the photo you are Jackie Kennedy:
black hair, that sway of the hips, the dress and jacket
you must have made in the evenings after work,
having cooked and cleared away, got the boys to bed,
your husband watching the evening news.
                              You stand
at the dining table, pinning the paper pattern
onto the glazed cotton, reach around
for the big dressmaking scissors, in your head

the plan to do what you've always wanted, walk
along a ward, the sunlight coming slantwise
through the long windows to a glass of water.
You knew who you were: not Jackie Kennedy,
one rich man after another: your orphaned self
on a street in a small dull town, in black and white
and the confidence you could mimic till it existed.

a ship sets out from Cyprus or Lebanon
cargo of olives logs tin terebinth

thirty-four centuries on
still undelivered

and cobalt glass

colour extinguished in
the deepsea dark

finding its glow at last
by the grace of divers

porcelain merchant
wrecked on a desert coast

his crew build a new boat
he heaps up stones

ships back an evening sky
to an inland town

looks for that lode again
but the beach has vanished

Exiled to the north, a cottage on a hill,
a view along the valley, an old milltown,
canal, Methodist chapel, the hospital
fifteen miles away on a snowy road.
You left the car at the bottom and hauled your shopping;
the next time harnessed the dog to a sled, came home
victorious, like Scott of the Antarctic.

                                        mined in Persia
along the Gulf across the Indian Ocean
                                            Sumatra China

                                     to be dragons phoenixes lions
                                              the eight immortals

                                              a sparrow on a branch
                                              a straight blue border

                                        black on the tip of the brush
                                                put to the flame

                emerging bluer than oceans bluer than summer

When your best friend's son, a few days out of prison,
sat on his bed wrapped in the counterpane
and put the gun to his head, you were the one

she phoned. You'd given up
for more than a year, but that day she handed you
one after another, lit, when you took a break
and went back in to clean the blood and flesh
off the furniture, carpet, ceiling.
                                                It's only now,
after the first of the strokes, you've had to stop
smoking again: just the one, you tell me,
last thing at night, and first thing in the morning.

                       grey northern light   grey sea
                                    silences plainsong

                            then a sea-crossing a sky
                                spires above cornfields

                colour   trapped from the wind
                                      scattered on stone

                          meaning not joy not faith
                                not the mother missing

                      toccata and fugue   a touch
                                    escape from being

When I came to the hospital it couldn't be
you in the blue flowered gown, with thin grey hair
greasy against your scalp, and dentures missing.
You, you kept insisting. *You. No, you,*
no other words with the strength to clamber out
into the bewildered overcrowded air.
You looked at the gifts I'd brought – lavender handcream,
expensive chocolates – as if they might have been
dug from an Iron Age fort in the chalk downland.
The words are mostly back, and the understanding;
though sometimes in your hand the TV remote
becomes inscrutable, the coloured buttons
arrows and icons an archaic language
that one day may open and reveal its function –
a list of grave-goods, prayer to the moon goddess –
though until then it's hard for the news to reach you.

           denser than summer sky
           more matte than water

           colour to lean against
           to gaze   no answer

indifferent god   that blocks
           absolution   meaning

           surface as deep as truth
           solid as grieving

What you have lost is still there, only hidden
like cobalt in a mountain, kobold, goblin,
trickster, disguised in copper, shape-shifter,

that goes into the furnace a black powder
and comes out radiant, butterfly, dragon, dolphin.

Alabaster

When he got ill, she took to carving things:
a fallen branch became a Gothic saint,
black stone, a pair of eagles. He could walk,
but slowly, from the door to the front gate.

Sculpture was all removal, hollowing out.
A carer came to take him for a bath,
dress him and shadow him around the house.
It was less shaming. She began to sand

and polish alabaster, first a form
like a Cycladic goddess, then a bowl.
He had come home again from hospital,

but not for long, they said. The open shell,
fluted, transparent, needed hours of work.
She sat beside him and he fell asleep.

Smoke

This very moment you are flying back

>   Sunday morning in February   thin cloud
>   and the smoke of a wood-burning stove
>   rising to smudge the blue

sealed and labelled
in a cardboard box in the hold
of a Swissair passenger plane
banking over the lake and its tower of water
the snow and the skiers

>   turning right across the countries that you won't
>   visit again   that we crossed years ago
>   on a train   heading off to find an island

but you can't see them
through the curved steel of the plane the box the plastic
container they call an urn
and anyway

what is there of you to see them   only ash
which used to be your bones   the rest of you

>   already risen into the Swiss sky
>   smoke from a you-burning stove
>   disseminated

in infinitesimal particles across
Geneva the French border the same woods
and villages you are flying above this minute

>   and a child looks up from a steep street

so now I find
surprisingly a cinder of compassion
somewhere inside me   you had no idea
how it would stop   your usual Christmas break

    best not to have known it

to set out   dapper as ever   clipped white beard
black cashmere winter coat   anticipating
walks and mulled wine and damask hotel evenings

    and return so diminished

Afterwards

so you got back into the limo and were driven
    what luxury out past the willow-trees and gravestones
        onto the by-pass
            left her

you thanked the driver
    and the undertaker in his penguin-suit
        and went
            inside for a stiff drink

thank heavens that's over you didn't say

while she was commuted
    the way they commute a prison sentence
        from life into only twenty years

from a very difficult person but aren't we all
    into smoke   along with her clothes her coffin
        the embalming fluid   which is formaldehyde

into bits of bone and finally into ash

while you were sitting in her chintz wing-chair
    thinking what happens next then
        there were no
            funeral meats no neighbours no relatives

only you and a future to get used to
    without her to tell you you were selfish shameless stupid
        though of course by now you could do it for yourself

while she was poured into a plastic urn
    and labelled and put on a shelf in the crem basement

you could have left her in the shrimping pools
    in the tideline seaweed tangled like wet knitting
        on the slippery rocks at the end of Dark Lane

but in those days nobody talked about scattering

so she carried on emanating across the fields
    railway lines concert halls you'd built between you

and you went back to work
    as if everything had happened
        but it made no difference

The Calabash

Gone midnight. A hard frost. Everyone asleep.
The goddess of forgetting
floats in off the street.

Very tall, and gaunt. Nothing she confiscates
nourishes her. Still she keeps on trying,
dropping objects into the pocket of her apron,

a book, a pair of earrings, yesterday's
walk to the shops. Already she's gnawed away
the coating of feeling:

fear, the man with the motorbike who kept
stopping three yards ahead of you and waiting;
shame, when you made it back. At least she's left you

the facts, so far. The goddess of forgetting
is pale and very old, with long stained teeth
that show when she smiles; not often, but it means

she's marked you now, the one with in the bedroom
an African batik, a woman walking
through a forest at night, carrying on her head
a calabash full of herbs and mysteries.

Transhumance

From the Swiss border down along the Rhône
and into the narrow lane through the chestnut woods
of the Massif des Maures, a bubbling blethering
breaker of white fleece around a bus
at night, on an old stone bridge, the headlights dimmed,
silence inside, the driver sitting back
and outside the shepherds, tall, walking and calling.

One day, not so far into the future
that I couldn't count the days if I sat down
at my desk in the grey light of a Sunday morning,
it will all start flowing
away, the word *transhumance* and the sheep
pouring down to the plain. I won't remember
the time for breakfast or my lover's name

nor how I got here, transmigration of souls
from the child abandoned in the empty ward.
Then what is left of me will be the moment,
exquisite in its colours and modulations,
the touch of glass on my fingertips, the scent
of hyacinths in a pot on the window-sill:
intensity I've wanted all these years

and useless because I'll no longer have the words
to turn it into a poem, to make it say
anything about my own life or the lives
of people shut the wrong side of a wall,
their olive trees on the other side still shaking
silver leaves in the wind, the olives swelling
and falling onto a net on the dry ground
to shrivel and rot, unharvested, untasted.

On the Esplanade

Pitched-roofed, piss-smelling, aching with slatted seats,
the shelter stares at the sea through salt-rimmed eyes,
a refuge from the sun and the shrieking children,
the sea-wind that pushes you over and runs off screaming,
the seagulls' raucous laughter and mocking cries.
You think in your youth you escaped, but once you're lying
immobile, hopefully drugged, you'll be freighted back
and propped on a bench in here, facing the waves,
the dachshund Cerberus sniffing at your shoes,
a quid in your hand for the fisherman in his boat,

as the tide moves in, over the seaworm trails,
over the rockpools, the seahorses and shrimps,
breached ramparts of abandoned sandcastles
and clambers the pebble-bank. Your soul will rise
arthritically, slowly, out of its puppet frame
and hobble forward, lean on the silver rail,
as the breaker roars, tosses its spindrift mane,
lumbers you into the safety of its throat.

The Inshore Waters

I

all water inland   silent   do not disturb
the shoremen at their hedging and ditching dreams
you could drown in this stuff   lingeringly   a dancer
past the leap of his youth   your port-de-bras superb

the staithe then the river   channels across the marsh
basalt   molten but cold   all unmet depth
paralysed motion   weedless   no pulse no splash

as if it were flowing backward   as if the waves
might thicken and surge between the reeds   upstream
the low pale sun catch a silky flash of green
on the throat of a breaker before it broke   you've seen
just such a choker glint at a beach and gone

II

What use to the world is water that thinks it's stone?
When you choose to drown
you'll have to get into a rowing-boat and make
oar-scars on the polished surface. You're facing back
to the staithe you left, willows and reeds. It's miles
to the sea from here. You're flagging. You pull the sculls
across your thighs, rest, float; but the water wants
to haul you in to the bank. Far off, in front
(if you turn your head) there's a bit of sheen in the sky,
a taste of salt to the cloudscape, so you try
again for the open ocean. A starting swell
rocks your coffin-cradle. Keep going. You'll do well
to reach the sea before sunset, but the dark's
just as good to drown in. That isn't a meadow-lark
or a seagull crying, it's you as you smell the tide,
as you hear the scrape of the shingle. Now, decide:
do you sit in your boat till it's toppled, or pull in
to the riverbank, step out to the sea wind
and the sky, the breakwaters, the flying spindrift –
if it ever was stone – fire-opal and amethyst.
A breaker rises and roars at you. Safe at last,
you pour down its throat.

III

You won't do it of course, walk into the sea and drown.
More likely a bout of asthma, a derailed train.
Though if one day it comes to it, the cancer back,
some antibiotic-resistant inward muck,
you'd do something to finish, you hope. Not a rowing-boat:
you've never learned to row anyway. No note
to whoever was going to find you in your bed
or more likely, sprawled on the kitchen floor. So you could
buy a one-way ticket down to some drab resort,
walk into the waves. Get a tide-table first,
you don't want to be striding out across the sand,
the water knee-high for miles; you might change your mind,
which isn't the point. Or is it? But are you brave,
could you keep on walking deeper until the waves
felled you and held you under? You'd hold your breath
as it spun you below the surface. It seems that death
may not come when you call. Or you have to yell
again, at the top of your lungs, before they fill.

III

Commander in Chief

What he does now is purify, the way you'd take
a rabble of rats in the drains, a swarm of germs,
e-coli, out of a clinic: historic task
he was born to, sworn to, his duty. He won't make
the error of doubt, the falter of counting cost,
as they shout he should, politicians in hygiene masks,
in their conference cant and smirking. They'll atone
for their treachery later. He watches as houses burn,
as hospitals with their load of the limbless rot.
Another dead child from the rubble. The diggers groan
and he does too, but privately, having lost
the right to lament. The schoolteachers are hiding
their lies in a cellar classroom. A barrel-bomb
grips through the ground, their fear and his might colliding.

What I Am Saying

the children come to school under the street
we wait for the phone call   drive towards the smoke
wrap a child in a cloth and carry her from the rubble
her face under the cloth
the rubble groaning

                              are you listening
                         can you hear the houses falling
                   in on themselves like giving up like loss
                       can you hear my shoes on the stones
                                            is this a city

today I bought bread that's all   the hospital
hungry   its mouth wide open   we can't take
the wounded there any more   the hospital
has gone   can you hear the doctors dying

                    are you listening   who are you anyway
                      what can you hear   is the generator on
                is the radio working   can you charge your phone
           can you see through the smoke   do you know what I am
                                                          saying

During the Bombing of Aleppo

starlings over Dunwich
an urgent message from the deleted city

swirling themselves into an alphabet
cursive   tidal

over Dunwich Heath

all that remains of people hurrying
to market   to get home before their children

starlings writing their bulletins on the sky
as it changes colour   sapphire   pale yellow   charcoal

The Martyrs of the Iran–Iraq War

They stare down at the cars they might have driven,
changing lanes too fast, making
a sudden right turn
into an alley with mud-brick walls that leaned
towards them and pulled down shade
and closed on darkness.

Girls in their day were never so beautiful,
they think, as these with their bright scarves
slipping back on black hair.
They could have arranged to meet in the Paradise Garden,
Bagh-e Eram, on a bench by the water-course
or under the redbud trees, the high blossom

almost the colour of the life they saw
draining into the desert. They could have been
dignified at the weddings of their children,
arguing politics, worrying over money,
or laughing with their friends (all also dead)
in the shade of a park, over tea and backgammon.

Hostile Environment

The tigers wait outside the villages.
The crocodiles wait below the water-lilies.
I've waited twenty years for permission to live here.

The informers wait in shaded alleyways.
The soldiers wait tetchily at the border.
I am waiting for my landlord to evict me.

The dictator waits for signs of disagreement.
His supporters wait to shoot at demonstrators.
I am waiting for my child's school to report me.

The traffickers wait for someone to pay a ransom.
The fisherman waits for his boat to come back empty.
I am waiting for the bank to withhold my money.

The children wait for a lorry to hide and die in.
I am waiting for you to decide to send me back.

Dawn Chorus

every morning   birdsong
    every morning   this morning   sky
       like a sheet on the line
    smelling of air although
early this morning

the sky not yet rinsed clean   the blackbird
    digesting a worm   someone
       woke to pounding
    on the door downstairs   someone
found himself taken

in a well-marked van
    along the street and out
       of the city   so someone
    left at home can't hear
    the blackbird singing   for
her children crying

the bird   in profile   on its usual
    rowan tree branch   doesn't do politics
       the blackbird acts only in its own
    self-interest   sex and competition
it hasn't chosen its song   although it's seen

a person taken away in manacles
    a person who used to look
       up at the tree every morning   and walk on
    a person who stopped of an evening with a child
saying *Listen*   *a blackbird*   in his human language

A Temporary Cease-Fire Has Been Negotiated

I wanted to go walking in the hills.
The streets were steep, a goods-train
groaned through the station.
After the houses there was only rock,
white rock and dark-green bushes, juniper.
The clouds were rocks upended on the sky,
and far below the sea shivered in silence.

A boat. Is it coming in to harbour
or stepping out onto the middle sea
round which the countries gather, wringing their hands?

The River at Tottenham Hale, below Ferry Lane

Old woman, like the Thames barges
moored sail-less beside the black-and-white
lock and its sluices; I have served my time

carrying hope downriver to hopelessness,
carrying gunpowder from the powder-mill
to those with the power to fire.
There was a boy

in a group of boys, late evening on the towpath,
with bikes and banter,
the mother putting the youngest son to bed
on the living-room sofa,
sisters with homework, Instagram, ambition,

still young enough for ambition. There was a boy
cycling fast from the police along the towpath,
bearing down on pedals, bent over handlebars
in the race in the dark. There was
suddenly a hole in the black water

that healed at once.
I am an old woman
scrawling my grief on the cold October morning,
graffiti on the houses, fried-chicken shops, while the boy

stock-still, is lying in a cold steel drawer,
lungs sodden with the inflow of river water,
duckweed staining his feet,
and in his muscles

the mornings he might have known,
the friends, the lovers,
the work of his hands,
the words he could have written.

An old woman whispers *NO!* across the streets
the estates, the deaths, the place where a bus once burned,

on the silent burning air
to the weeping river.

Today, Tomorrow

an elegy

This morning the fish-man lays out the white boxes
on his stall at the corner as usual: river trout,
red mullet, prawns; as usual the greengrocer
calls *Two for a pound!* and the sports-shop manager
bends to unlock the metal blind, which rises
out of her sight like a ladder into heaven.

The shoppers begin to arrive, stepping off buses,
coming down in the lift from the carpark: determined women
followed by shopping-trolleys like tired retrievers;
couples with buggies. A man in an anorak
hunkers down on his cardboard by the cash machine,
the Witnesses set up their stand outside the station.
Girls screech at each other like herring-gulls,
boys stroll in their white trainers. A day passes.

*

Who is the patron saint of teenagers?
Which pagan god protects them? Stall the buses!
Block Lordship Lane to pedestrians and traffic!
Let it rain in torrents, thunderstorms distract them,
hailstones batter and bruise the knifing arm,

and it won't have happened. Where were you, blindfold Justice,
where were you, Mercy? Why did you give these children
not bread but a stone, not home but a crowded room
with damp and despair? Wisdom, why did you tell them
they were nothing, could be nothing but blades of vengeance?

*

The blood that just now was speeding through his veins,
pulsing his heart, is washed into the gutter.
His body's gone
to the hospital, in the yellow ambulance.
The boys have gone,
skeetered away from the screams, the onlookers,

their power and their own terror. Tomorrow morning
the children will come with roses wrapped in plastic
bartered from Lidl and the market trader
for all their savings; tomorrow a dune of flowers.
Tomorrow the people waiting at the bus stop
will wander over to see, and the bus will come
and take them away, shaken. Today at home
his sister opens the door to the policewoman.

VI

A Grenfell Alphabet

A lament

Floor 1
In the burning high-rise hive there are alphabets,
Arabic Tamil Ge'ez, there are apricots
brought from the market
today for their flame-soft skin, and animals,
real animals, a jerbil, a terrapin
its tank-water heating up
don't think of that.

Floor 2
Think instead about birthday-cards, a shelf
with a whole year of good wishes, and books of course,
school-books, novels, encyclopaedias
left by a grandfather, Haynes manuals,
gardening books for the allotment farmers,
books printed in faraway alphabets,
Hindi Cyrillic Chinese, yes, lots of books.

Floor 3
A cuckoo-clock, clock-radio, the time
burning away don't think of that, the time
consumed already. Carrots, cucumbers,
coriander in plastic flower-pots, cumin seeds
giving life its savour, heating up, the scent
wanders into the stairwell with the smoke
and the sound of steps in the dark, the thud on stairs.

Floor 4
Dishes are washed and drying in racks, there are dinners
kept in the fridge for tomorrow, there are doorbells,
Westminster chimes to ring you into England
to London to Ladbroke Grove after all that travel
all that escape, doorbells on doors that aren't
fireproof in spite of the fire brigade.

Floor 5
There are eggs in racks in the fridge, that would have been
breakfast tomorrow, there are eiderdowns
pulled up to cover the ears, Elastoplast
printed with dinosaurs, cans of rose emulsion
to embellish the bedroom, and eagles, red and black,
two-headed, staring out from the mantelpiece,
much of the time forgotten.

Floor 6
                                 Forget-me-nots
on the birthday cards and the get-well cards,
and fabrics, woven and knitted, everywhere,
on cushions, in upholstery and curtains,
clothes hanging in wardrobes, overalls
ready for work tomorrow, summer dresses
and babies' bibs in a drawer. Fabrics are what
humanity is made of.

Floor 7
                      Look, the gifts
received and put on show, humanity
is a giver of gifts, a book, a Playstation,
gold necklace bracelet and earrings, wedding set,
and gifts still wrapped from the shop, due to be given
tomorrow perhaps, so the heart lifts, the thought
of pleasure soon to be felt and understood
don't think of that, receiver and giver lost
along with the gift, yes, think of it, the givers
and makers, goldminers, silk-weavers,
all the givers of the world among the flames.

Floor 8
Think of the hats. Black uniform peaked cap,
best Sunday churchgoing hat with scarlet flowers,
starched head-tie, Sikh turban, can we call
a turban a hat? Think about the headscarves,
face-framing hijab, and fascinators,
all net and feathers, sun-hats, Panamas
brought back from the Caribbean. Holidays
past and to come, with brochures, souvenirs,
photos, forgotten lovers, reunions,
all the aunts and second cousins waiting at home.

Floor 9
Ice-cream in freezers, pistachio, as good
as at home or almost, irises in bright
prints on the bedroom wall. iPad, iPlayer
the programmes missed but available another
month into the future don't think of that.
Think instead of icons,
saints wide-eyed at the martyrdom, their own
hallowed pain in gold-leaf, haloes in flames.

Floor 10
June warm at last, light evenings, jubilation,
jobs on minimum wage and zero hours
but jobs at least. Jehovah's Witnesses
Jesuits Jews jazz-singers jet-skiers
all lifting up their eyes unto the hills
from whence cometh no help. Don't think of that.
And was Jerusalem builded here? Don't answer.

Floor 11
The keyring always hung behind the door,
the kettle filled at night for early coffee.
Ketchup in bottles, children's karate-clothes.
Kaleidoscope, a hundred and twenty-nine
silent bedrooms at once, red or gold curtains,
navy or emerald clothes on yellow chairs.
Kali, mother
red-eyed with rage, creator and destroyer,
why didn't you wake these people as you woke
Vishnu when he was needed to fight the demons?

Floor 12
London exists in tube-maps, Oyster-cards,
landline numbers, addresses on envelopes,
Latimer Road and Ladbroke Grove, the stations.
Longing, for long-lost family, long past
successes, friendships, happiness. Long hair,
brown blonde or black, plaited or lying loose
across the pillow, across the sleeping arm
of the loved or unloved other, lesbian,
gay straight or happy with anyone
loving enough for an evening or to live with.

Floor 13
Mattresses. The mattress on the floor
of the empty flat, no sheets, a blue blanket,
a mound of clothes needing washing. Melancholy.
Must go out, must hide from Immigration,
must work, send money home. At least there's music,
maracas, mandolins, Mozart, melodies
heard in the street, meandering in the head
in the insomniac hours, ska, heavy metal,
rai, ragas, Ethio-jazz, don't fall asleep.

Floor 14
Everyone here counts in their first language,
nine nëntë neuf navad. There are mobile numbers
stored in phones, with names, sometimes with photos.
Same-storey neighbours
met in the morning on the way to work
to the school the nursery. So, nursery-rhymes
in as many languages, rhymes to enchant the children,
to chant on the way to the playground: goats and sheep,
princesses, giants and shepherds, nasty monsters.

Floor 15
Of course there have to be ovens, every flat
equipped with its own oven, a microwave
or a proper oven, everyone needs to cook,
even the person dossing on the mattress
in the empty flat. There has to be an opal,
a greenish one, set in a silver ring.
What's the melting point for opal before it flows
out of its setting and becomes an ocean,
sunset on water, blue-green, a touch of red
for the flames flickering up don't think of that,
a sea where the opal-owner remembers floating.

Floor 16
Pianos penny-whistles postage-stamps.
Someone writes home, where they don't have internet.
Someone plays a tune over and over
till someone else protests or praises them
or simply listens, the tune is slowly slowly
forming itself out of the memory
of the old heard tune, into a breath, a movement
of hands and breathing, so someone coming in
from the park the market hears it and sings along.

Floor 17
Questions, questions
that people ask themselves or knock on doors
to ask each other, people write their questions
on council websites, in emails, people speak
yes think of that, a paper-pile of questions
in the corner of an office, in an in-tray
under piles of other questions. People save
a copy at home in a box-file. Paper burns.

Floor 18
Roses on duvet-covers on pencil-cases,
pink roses on a dress on a child's hairband,
rose-patterned rug in a sitting-room, a vase
of real pink roses on a dining-table,
a few open already, one bud bent
down to the table in shame, already grieving.

Floor 19
Shadow on the wall as a plane passes
between the sun and the window, sound arriving
planing the sky to smooth, like a lens-grinder
polishing a mirror to see the stars,
uncover the truths of the universe. What's seen
from the top floors of the tower, the sky making
clouds out of steam that rises from rain-forests,
snow out of frozen sunlight, snow-crystals
tumbling through vapour-trails, always something falling.

Floor 20
Tea is what is offered. Everyone,
however newly arrived or penniless,
when a neighbour knocks has a cup of tea to offer.
With milk, with lemon,
in mugs, in painted glasses, teabags, loose
tea in the tea-caddy someone's auntie left them
that she bought in a junk-shop, that someone brought
all the way home in his kitbag after the war.

Floor 21
Underneath you are hundreds of people, and you are under
more floors more ceilings, the roof with the safety door
that's no use to you now. The underdog
is not who you feel you are, but when they make you
apply for jobs you can't take because of the children,
produce your papers in front of the customers
wasting their lattes and watching you being questioned,
you know you're under stress duress suspicion,
out in monsoon, umbrella left at home.

Floor 22
Visitors sleep on the sofa for a few
nights when they come for a wedding, a few weeks
while they wait to hear from the Home Office. Vacant flats
are not filled fast enough, though everyone
knows someone who ought to live here. Vocal chords
violinists vegans voters need vaccinating
against political venom, which blows in
from the spluttering mouths of venal politicians.

Floor 23
Wheelchairs are good for moving with the times,
around the flat and out onto the street
as long as the lifts are working, which isn't often.
Walking sticks help but you're slow. You never wanted
to be deprived of waltzes windmills waterfalls
the West End and Walthamstow, but you make a home
of your home, the plate-glass windows and the stars.

Floor 24
X the unknown number of the victims.
Y the question nobody wants to answer.
Z for the zero that is Grenfell Tower
now, its missing windows and scorched stairs,
zero the objects that can still be salvaged,
zero the rooms it would be safe to enter.
Zeus, Zoroaster,
in the zenith above the charred black tower, who welcomed
the singing souls that rose out of the flames?

V
Lethe

Not Like This

I choose to remember him at the conference
First we have to listen to each other;

in refugee week
in Kennington Park, moving among the plane trees,
the Colombian dancers, sellers of necklaces;

dancing at the end of a long meeting,
a big man shimmying to a djembe rhythm;

or in my old flat
in front of the coal fire, lifting
my feet to rest either side of his throat.

Only not
lost in his own known streets.

Not lost.
Not lost.

Before We Knew

As if the sea had given up on change,
high tide every day at the same time
reaching half up the shingle,
and no wild
drenching over the sea-wall, no house shaking –

I'd lost him already. Or rather, I was bored.
Like a calm sunlit sea he was sweet and loving,
and talked about Brixton market and politics,
same words every time,

and sometimes he forgot we were meant to meet,
as if the sea had suddenly withdrawn,
as we know it can before a devastation,

but there was no crash,
no vast green breaker rearing like a dragon.

All the destruction had already happened.

Prometheus

Not chained to his rock;
bound there by gentleness and explanation
till he can hardly picture the walk away

into the valley, olive-trees, oleander,
a goat-bell singing, beehives, a village dance.
How he once loved dancing.

Not chains but fear,
not the eagle clawing his flesh but obedience.
There are things he no longer knows, and he can't be sure
they won't swoop towards him, hungry and menacing.
He thinks he was
generous once,

what he gave: his thoughtfulness and his still patience
and the message:
We all have our pain.
Listen to the stories.

Where has it gone, that dignity and purpose?
He longs to walk
away from the rock into the healing sunlight,

fears he'd never discover the footpath home.

Bees

But now, and here
Is night's short forgiveness
That all lovers use.
Keith Douglas

That night: a cold hotel room,
clinging together under shifting blankets,
and oh, what wouldn't we give
for even that racket
of window-frame and storm,
that sleepless torment,

now that the air is hot and the nights mild,
the call of a fox
here, and maybe for you,
twelve miles away, at four am, a blackbird.

Now not even an afternoon
with the white blind trembling,
laughter of the child in the next door garden,
our hands knowing
what the other's body longs for.
Nothing travels

between us now; not even
the bees in my garden,
nuzzling up to the bluebells, are permitted
to whirr across London,
deliver their gift of pollen, fall asleep.

Redevelopment

You've become the sliced end of a house,
upstairs a tapering chimney-breast, soot on brick,
the walls blue eggshell, a door
that must have been painted white, a handle-hole.

You are my memory of who you were,
and sometimes you remember: a holiday
beside the Med with your children, a conference
you chaired, coaxed enemies to conversation.

Someone who once was a child in the lost house
walks past, looks up at the trace of a mantelpiece
on the painted wall, thinking, Yes, that was us,
but doesn't know it for certain, hurries home.

Pigeon Post

You know me
better than that

don't you
as if I'd let you

dwindle
a shadow past

my bay window at night
a phonograph

crackle and hiss
as if I'd let your kiss

dry on my mouth

*

It's curfew
lockdown   but

I send my heart
racing-pigeon   out

over office blocks
all the lights turned off

over the river   bridge
straining across

to wait at your bedroom window
till the sun

levers it open
you are still asleep

on your side
as if

I curled
in the gap

    *

Did you think I would
leave you to chance

to virus
to come to grief

My heart has brought
your memory

leaves the box
on the pillow beside you

My heart has lost heart

out of breath
doesn't have

the heart to fly back

Ghost Station

I confess   I imagined you all along
you strode out of midday
bougainvillea   ocean   out of myth

I didn't see you
you said
not as much as I love you
you knew I was

rose absorbed in its scent
elaborate rose absorbed in its unfolding

that remembers the gardener
only when he withholds
nutrients   water

*

I am forbidden to see you
they say you are
vulnerable

you with your strong shoulders
your silences   they mean
to the virus
I think you are
unarmed against me

I am a rose absorbed by its own thorn

they say the illness
lounges on the back seat of the bus
travels the tube
grasping the rail next to the opening doors

I cannot see you

lost confused you write
we have lost each other

in the empty tunnels at night
among the paper
blowing along the tracks
the city's rodents

*

the rosebush shakes in the wind
there is more here
than you and I in the city

in the unlit tunnel
the rats tear at the litter
I walk and walk
between the live rail and the looming brick

here is an echo
once it was a station

now a tangle of cables against a wall
posterless platform

lifts lifted out of their cage
the breezeblocked exit

Intertidal

where light
sleeks down the mud
to satin bedding

                                          sleep here!
                            gives under your step
                               won't give you up

where starfish slide away
oystercatchers
vigil

                                              sea-urchins
                           put up their sea-defences
                                   redshanks siren

where they buried the witch
under a slab
in case
death didn't work

                             where what you've lost
                                the word for son
                                     his name
                             who it is you love

have slid
into the silt

stand here on the bank
where once...

                                                 the tide
                                    lurches back in
                                          hides

fossils
rotted stanchions
the bones of boats

VI

Tidal

Far end of the land. The lullaby of water,
hush, hush, to the pebbles, to the shells
fracturing into sand. Hush, there is no
panic in this, no doubting it. The dark
wraps its shawl around your shoulders, the salt air
tautens your skin. Far out ahead of you
where a horizon might hover, a single light,
a fishing-boat or a vagrant planet. Stay
still, stay silent, listen to the words
the tide brings in on its sweep from the Antarctic,
the protest of the seagulls before they too
close into sleep. Listen. Even the seaweed
caught in on itself, tangled, trying to reach
the seawall, has its sonnet for you to write.

Moorings

Head towards water. This is a landing-stage
for whatever you want: dew, willow, a tufted duck
if you're lucky, a scrattle of thistle-heads, a squirrel,

a poem, slipping in mildly off the broad
inarticulate river. Turns off its outboard, floats
on a basalt ripple, docks by a boat called Blott

and one called Spirit of Solace. If you stand
here at the edge it'll throw you its mooring-rope.

If You Want Thunder

Then sometimes people ask you how it was,
and what you see's a pale green corridor,
blood dripping out of you, the man who swore
it wouldn't hurt, and hurt you. Just because
you could tell no-one (shame) you can't say now
where you have been, or why. The simple answer:
It's past, I've changed. You wouldn't want to squander
scarce memory on the prurient, anyhow.

So time spreads blankness, like an overcast
November morning, mild, an even light
over the park, the pond, the lime-tree walk.
That backlit terror disappeared as fast
as lightning sketched across an autumn night.
If you want thunder you must learn to talk.

Self-Portrait with Skull

Could have been carved from the chalk downs:
long scarp to the muzzle, yellow-white,
flint-blue, plus rust and mud. Among harebells, gorse
ploughed fields, a skim of umber,
bone wearing through. I can't
do landscape any more. One of the children
found it, up on the Ridgeway; and I thought

memento mori, *The Ambassadors*. Arrogance!
Brittle, pared away, and the window-light
colours it earthwards. Imagine it galloping
against the skyline. Grins now. Such confidence.
For centuries. I was a painter, once.
I sit for myself. Empty-handed. Cobalt dress.

Grünewald

To make water flow wherever it's told, you need
a wooden box with four divining-rods,
a compass, several men with boots and shovels,
a pump to shift it by its own volition,
and me, Meister Mathis, hydraulic engineer,
clerk-of-works, model maker, stonemason,

also painter of many-hinged altar-pieces,
so men and women with St Anthony's
sacred fire charring their blood and skin
stare and are healed. I work in tempera
I mix myself, with just a little oil
so the colour goes on clear, like a held note

on an angel's trumpet: here it's cinnabar,
red mercury. Jesus dies,
his whole weight hanging from his nailed-up hands,
blood from his head wounds; but when the fathers turn
the panels outward on feast-days, his linen shroud
flames in the up-draught of his resurrection.

I observe where I am, and paint: the leering faces,
green skin, festering lesions, how the sinful
imagine their souls. For the Last Supper,
I sit the ungainly tired apostles round
an oval table, in twos and threes, arguing,
and Christ the least of them, or the least human,

already half disincarnate. At the far end,
fingertips pressed together in explanation,
is my namesake, Mathis, Matthew the tax collector,
a clever man, used to working out the cost,
already glimpsing the next afternoon
when the sky will darken and the saints' graves open.

One Day the Poets Will Return to Earth

and sit on a park bench
  with sealed eyes

to let the unstable sun
  burn off their fever

*

sound of a door unlocked
    a voice calling

the poets running downstairs
    hello? where are you?

*

a battered cardboard box
  humming   vibrating

bees returning home
  to a city pavement

*

three roses in a vase
    disintegrate

the darkened fallen parts
  still singing perfume

*

a wicker coffin
with a crown of lilies

coffin in flames in its kiln
  lilies in sunlight

For Eavan Boland

I've been reading your last book.
It's not yet light,

but a bird on the lamp-post
has been singing since I got up before seven

when the air was even darker, not a sky
but an absence of co-ordinates, a warning.

You didn't know that book would be your last.
In the poems apples fall on a wet lawn,

a gate opens, a child
comes running towards you as one always did,

your daughters and now their children, who are seeing
the easing of the morning to indigo,

to January, which sets
the headstone of LAST YEAR on the way you died

suddenly, your hair no longer bright
red-gold as it was for many years, your voice,

its music in this slate-blue winter night.

The Painted Sky

In the middle of life's journey, I was eating
fish and chips in a motorway service station,
when from somewhere near the door I heard a greeting,

my name and birthplace, and an invitation
to go outside, exploring. I was scared
but tried to justify my hesitation:

'But I've just got here,' and I turned towards
the speaker, a tall woman, dressed in grey,
her face in shadow. 'Yes,' she said, 'it's hard

to leave so soon, but on the motorway
things tend to happen quickly.' So I stood
and followed her, out by a hidden way

past bins and smokers, to a plank of wood
unpainted, laid across a shallow stream.
'Stand in the centre'; then a cotton hood

was dropped over my face. 'I know it seems
unfeeling now,' she murmured, 'but you'll see
more clearly when we get there.' You know in dreams

you move abruptly, from beside a tree
into a pub and then a flower-bed?
That's how it was that afternoon for me.

I was trying to remember what she'd said
and what it meant for me; but I was standing
in a palace room, gold, azure, dusky red,

staring at frescoes of a woman handing
a goblet to a woman. I was both
and the painted sky and the eagle soaring, landing.

The Aralqum Desert

male eighty
five foot nine
hospital gown

3 January 10 am
to shelf A7

4 Feb to freezer unit
nobody's claimed him

not

his landlord
postman
barman

betting-shop manager
card-players
creditors

till a cousin-twice-removed
who's moved to Reading

spring morning
street trees flowering

the man melting

curtained viewing room
coffin lined

with plastic sheeting
in case
calico sheeting

lavender oil
can't shroud

the dissolution

*

Barsa-Kelmes
Land of No Return

once island
now desert
Aralqum

bleached seashells
broken boat-hulls

the one ranger

found seated
five years later
head in his hands

*

I woke in a god-size bed
with a goose-down duvet

sea bright-blue sonorous
through plate-glass windows

she was still alive
asleep
in another room
I didn't have to see her
I thought I might

inherit the cliff-top house
be rocked to sleep

each night by the loving water
in early morning

walk
into the sun-
and-spindrift blessing

*

Christmas cards
windowsill bookshelves dresser
red and glitter

fifty-two times my name
love
signatures

at fifty-two points
in space-time
recollected

*

new festival
Day of the Unwanted

whose fathers wiped their cocks and went downstairs

whose mothers couldn't pay for an abortion

bottle-fed
every four hours
by harassed nurses

a day to celebrate our resourcefulness
having no option

our courage
walking the grass
above the cliff

into the wind off the sea
our determined dying

Sonnet Written with a Pink Pen

My tiny hand is frozen, having cleaned
mould out of the fridge. I've scoured the loo,
made chicken soup, altered a pair of jeans,
addressed a meeting. It's what women do.

I've dressed a dead man in his football shirt
and laid him in his coffin; known the stench
we all may melt to; comforted the hurt
partners and enemies. I didn't flinch,

or not in public. For thirty years I've written
poems of death and exile, sex and grief,
Pinochet, Kosovo, London riots, love.
Now that I've got this pen, though, I can prove
my feminine vocation: violets, kittens,
cupcakes and curls. Imagine my relief.

The Boatman

believes in silence
only the oars' discussion with the waves
only the sigh as a duck lands on the river

which is ever wider
however often his arms lift and fall back
however cool the sun sings in the mist

Notes

Endangered
Serquais, a variety of Norman French, is the language of the island of Sark. In 2011 there were an estimated twenty speakers left.

Cobalt Variations
The details are taken from Edmund de Waal's *The White Road*.

The Calabash
Batik by Nike Davies-Okundaye.

What I Am Saying
Largely based on comments by a member of the White Helmets, volunteer paramedics in Syria.

During the Bombing of Aleppo.
Dunwich, in Suffolk, had a population of 3,000 at the time of the Domesday Book. It was destroyed by repeated storms in the thirteenth and fourteenth centuries, and most of its buildings are now under the North Sea. The population was 183 at the last census.

The Martyrs of the Iran-Iraq War
The faces of those killed in the war are displayed on banners all through the streets of Iran. The Paradise Garden is in Shiraz.

Hostile Environment
'The aim is to create, here in Britain, a really hostile environment for illegal immigrants,' Theresa May, 2012.

One Day the Poets Will Return to Earth
Based on a line from the French poet Jean Cassou, translated by Timothy Adès.

Self Portrait with Skull
Inspired by the painting of the same name by Juliet Wood.

Grünewald
Grünewald's altarpiece for the Antonite monastery at Isenheim is made of twelve double-hinged panels which can be opened or closed to give three composite views. The monastery was a hospice for people suffering from ergotism, known as holy fire or St Antony's fire.

The Aralqum Desert
This desert, in Kazakhstan, was once the seabed of part of the Aral Sea. Barsa-Kelmes, meaning land of no return, was an island in the Aral Sea, but now is part of the mainland.

Sonnet Written with a Pink Pen
For Valentine's Day 2016, Bic relaunched its pink ballpoint pen, designed specially to fit the hands of the ladies.

The Boatman
After the song by Nitin Sawney.

Acknowledgments

Thanks are due to the editors of the following publications where sone of these poems were first published – *Allegro, Blackbox Manifold, Compass, Ekphrastic Review, Smeuse* and *Glasgow Review of Books.*

'A Temporary Cease-Fire Has Been Negotiated' was printed as a gift card for subscribers to my chapbook *Rubaiyat for the Martyrs of Two Wars* (Hercules Editions, 2017). 'A Grenfell Alphabet' was first published as a pamphlet, to raise funds for the Grenfell Tower fund. It was recorded and published on *Emerging Voices* http://www.emergingvoices.co.uk.

Thanks to Seraphima Kennedy and the Lent Sonnets group; several of the poems here emerged from that forty-day discipline. And many thanks, as ever, to Caroline Maldonado for feedback on individual poems and the collection as a whole, and for years of friendship.